Braker's Rules for Contractors

Braker's Rules
for Contractors

First Edition

Roger Braker

http://RogerBraker.com
http://PovertyvsWealth.com

Thanks to my wife that greatly helped me in editing, and to the young man that inspired me to put this in writing. And I thank God without which I would still be an ignorant rube.

Contents

Preface

To run a successful contracting business, it is much like a game of chess. There is a great necessity to think through how you set up your business. You need a good set of common sense business rules to guide your decisions and your dealings with people. Braker's Rules for Contractors is a way of helping young contractors think about what they are doing and what they may need to change in their dealings with people to have continued success.

Accumulating rules that govern life are all part of The Prosperous Life.

Braker's Rules for Contractors

Never wish life were easier, wish that you were better. Jim Rohn

CHAPTER 1

The Reason for Braker's Rules for Contractors

The phone rings. "I need you to come look at a unit for a repair so I can take the quote to the loan closing." Me, "Our charge for looking at a unit is a set fee, and we need to be paid while we are there."

Rule #1 – We Charge to "Look."

I realized at that moment that I had a set of rules that I use to guide my business. I had just never thought of these principles as a set of rules, nor had I ever numbered them.

Rules to guide you through life are not uncommon. Everyone needs a code or set of rules to live by or conduct their business with.

An example of a rule of conduct: John Wayne in the movie, The Shootist, said, "I'll not be laid a hand on." Since his passing, his son has published a book called, John Wayne's Code. The Boy Scout oath is another example.

A very simple partial set of rules for life might include:

1. Going to bed and rising at the same time every day
2. Being kind to everyone I meet
3. Working from a to-do list as much as possible
4. Walking away from arguments whether in person or on-line as much as possible

George Washington had his <u>Rules of Civility</u> that he carried in his pocket as a young man, and we all know how well that turned out for him. Here are a few excerpts from his little book:

- # 6. Sleep not when others Speak, Sit not when others stand, Speak not when you should hold   your Peace, walk not on when others Stop.
- # 11. Shift not yourself in the Sight of others nor Gnaw your nails.
- # 19. Let your Countenance be pleasant but in Serious Matters Somewhat grave.
- # 51. Wear not your clothes, foul, ripped or dusty but see they be brushed once every day at least and take heed that you approach not to any uncleanness.
- # 56. Associate yourself with men of good quality if you esteem your own reputation; for tis better to be alone than in bad company.
- # 90. Being set at meat scratch not, neither spit, cough or blow your nose except when there's a necessity for it.

On the TV show <u>NCIS</u>, the main character has his own list of rules, too. The ones I like the best are:

- Never say you're sorry. It is a sign of weakness.
- Never go anywhere without a knife.
- Never, ever involve a lawyer.
- Sometimes you're wrong.

The more I thought about rules, I realized I had several that I used in my business. Others I talked to said they had learned the same lessons. But there was nowhere I knew of where a young person could find them listed. So I began to record and number them as they came up.

Rule #2 – We Charge for Every Trip.
(As much as possible)

Example: A customer called last week. His house had been struck by lightning and had knocked out the electronics on his unit. He wanted me to come look at it and write up an estimate for the repairs. I tried politely telling him we had a trip charge for that, and he would say, "Just write it up for the insurance, and we will turn it in." I finally had to explain bluntly that he would need to pay me the day I came. Then we could write up the rest and turn that in. He agreed. It works much better to tell people up front what you expect.

Now when the parts come, if it takes multiple trips, we expect payment before we leave **each** time.

The reason is that after you have "looked," or written up an estimate or given your advice, they may later decide to throw it away and start over, fix it themselves or whatever. Then you will have a hard time getting paid for anything at a later date.

You see many people look at contractors as low-lifes or fly by night outfits. They think they are doing you a favor by perhaps paying you **some** money for their job.

I have been told when I was younger to only enter through the back door, the servant's entrance.

I see my business as a business and run it that way. What they think they see is a man hoping to make enough money to pay his rent and buy food for the week. Now not everyone is like that, but a great many are. The solution is to conduct yourself according to a set of rules (which hopefully comes off with an air of confidence, instead of an air of hoping to make some money). Then also remember that the rules may not always apply. But they do apply 999 times out of 1000!

Accumulating rules that govern life are all part of The Prosperous Life.

Proverbs 14:24 The wise accumulate wisdom; fools get stupider by the day.
(The Message)

CHAPTER 2

Expect God To Give You The Right Words!

Rule #3 – Expect God to Give You the Right Words!

Many years ago, I had been doing warranty work for a manufacturer on some units for a builder. I repaired many of them, but I still did not do the builder's construction repairs. Finally, I got up courage to go talk to the owner of this large company. When I entered the room, he shook my hand, asked me to have a seat and said, "I wondered how long it was going to be before you came in. Of course, you can have all our work." I was amazed at how easy that was. He was waiting for me.

Many times in running a business or contracting, you run into situations with people that are just uncomfortable or that can cause fear or great apprehension in you.

I have learned over the years how to deal with some of these situations. I took much of the learning from the Bible and used it in my work.

1. Ask God to "give you mercy before the man." This comes from a record in Genesis where Joseph's brothers (loving brothers that they were) sold him off to some traveling merchants which took Joseph down into Egypt and sold him. Eventually, Joseph attained the position of second in command just under Pharaoh. It was in a great period of drought that under Joseph's direction, Egypt had plenty to eat and some to sell. Joseph's fa-

ther, Jacob, already thinking that his one son was dead to him sent all but one of his sons into Egypt to buy food for their family. They did not recognize Joseph, but Joseph did recognize his brothers. So Joseph gave them the food and sent them on their way, but he kept one of the brothers as a hostage until they would bring back his younger brother. Sometime later, Jacob now missing two sons (he did not know that Joseph was "the man" in Egypt), needed more food and sent his sons back again to Egypt and said the following to them as they departed.

Genesis 43:13-14 Take also your brother, and arise, go again unto the man: And **God Almighty give you mercy before the man,** that he may send away your other brother, and Benjamin. If I be bereaved *of my children,* I am bereaved.

I believe that this was Jacob's prayer to God. He asked God to show them mercy before the man. You could ask for this mercy from God in many situations. Here are a few:

1. Getting a call from an irate customer
2. Going in for an interview
3. Getting stopped by the police

I saw a video the other day talking about how the police treat people. If the policeman is having a good day and everything is lovely in his life, you may just get a warning. But if his wife has just called and told him she is getting a divorce, you may get taken to the station for the same offense. This is where asking God for mercy in front of the man is so important. People are just people. Their moods can differ from day to day. But God should know when you are going to be in the situation where you need some help. So ask God to give you the right person for the interview or have the only person available to be the one that will give you what you need -- jobs/contracts/ referrals etc., so you can slip right in. Ask God to show you mercy before the man.

2. Expect that God will bring you into favor with the people that can say "yes" to your business. This idea comes from the record in Daniel. Some of the children of Israel had been carried off as captives to the land of Babylon (present day Iraq). Some were to be educated in the ways of the Chaldeans so they could stand before the king as advisors. The prince of the eunuchs was put in charge of these men. (A eunuch is a man who has been castrated, especially (in the past) one employed to guard the women's living areas at an oriental court.) The eunuch really liked Daniel and the three other men as recorded here in Daniel.

Daniel 1:9 Now **God had brought Daniel into favour** and tender love with the prince of the eunuchs.

Many times you will find that the people that you contract with or work for really like you. How God does this I don't know but just be thankful. And realize that you can ask God to find favor in the minds of the people you work with. Or you could ask God to send clients that will be great to work for.

3. Expect God to give you the "Right words (wisdom) at the right time to resolve the situation."

This Idea comes from:

James 1:5-6 If any of you lack wisdom, let him ask of God, that giveth to all *men* liberally, and upbraideth not; and it shall be given him. But let him ask in faith, nothing wavering. For he that wavereth is like a wave of the sea driven with the wind and tossed.

When I first started out hanging wallpaper as a young man, I would get calls at times after I was done and was paid for a job that the customer was unhappy about something they saw in my work. Then I would have to go back to the job and deal with it.

So I would take a "B" Vitamin (supposed to help the brain function better) and ask God to give me the "right words at the right time to resolve the situation." Out of all the call backs I had in 25 years, I only had to redo a couple of screw ups. Many times it was the fault of the paper or the wall or it could have been a multitude of different circumstances. But they were unhappy, and we needed to resolve the situation.

I never asked God for me to come out on top, just for the situation to be resolved. I was not trying to stick anyone with a bad job by praying.

I remember one night I got a call from an irate husband after he saw the job his wife had paid for already. I prayed but was really nervous about going to talk to him. When I walked in the door, he started in on me and was railing for about five minutes. Finally, he began to calm down. Up to that point, I never said a word. Finally, he said, "I realize you probably could have done nothing about this; I just needed to get it off my chest. Thanks for listening." Then I left. God put the thought in me, "Just be quiet!"

On another job, the builder called and said that the lady was in tears because she could see the seams in the wallpaper. I told him he needed to get a manufacturer's representative to look at the job because there was nothing wrong with it. He said he knew it was a good job but the woman was crying anyway. So I took a can of colored pencils and chalk I had and went to see her. Now this was a cream colored paper with some trees on it that crossed at the seams. But mostly the seams were just cream colored with no pattern. I had no idea what to do. So I reached into the can of pencils and pulled out a charcoal pencil. I thought, "Well, that won't work on this background." But then I thought, "Well, it is the first thing you pulled out. Just try it." So I did, and as I ran the edge of the charcoal pencil up the cream colored seam, the seam just disappeared. To this day, I don't

know why that worked, but I do know that prayer is very helpful in resolving situations when you expect God to be involved.

Proverbs 2:7 He layeth up sound wisdom for the righteous...

CHAPTER 3

Never Back Up On A Bid!

Rule #4 – Never Back Up On a Bid!

When a young person first starts into business for themselves, their tendency is to underbid the jobs. This may be because of several reasons:

- They may feel somewhat inadequate or insecure.
- They may be afraid they will not get the job if they bid/price it higher.
- They may feel inferior to others that have been in that market for years.

Most people that continue this line of thinking either go out of business or go to work for someone that knows how to bid.

The problem with pricing below the market to secure some work is that the customers you will get are the ones that are concerned only with price. Later on when you want to raise your prices, you will lose these customers to some other low bidder and have to replace them.

A friend of mine and I did some landscaping on our days off many years ago. One thing he shared that his grandfather taught him was to price out the entire job at the market price then add 10%. So if the job was $3,000, it came out to $3,300. I have practiced this with great success for many years since then, and it also has the benefit of helping to keep your prices up and pushing higher. This also helps to keep you from under bidding a job.

Many times you will have unexpected expenses or time in a job, and now you have already priced that in. Without the extra 10%, you will feel gypped when the unexpected arises. This technique just helps cover your a**. You walk away after completion feeling satisfied.

Pity the man that, when confronted by the buyer about the price, backed up on the bid to $2500.00 or lower to get the job and then complications arise. Been there, done that, and we don't do that anymore. You walk away feeling slightly sick and disgruntled. Learn to walk away if they want a lower price. Many times they will call you back later. They were just testing your commitment to the price.

The only time I remember coming down on a bid was when the bid was $750.00. The client said that was too much and asked if I would do it for $650.00? God must have showed me it was OK because I never did this again. But this time I told him I could do $725.00, but that was it. He, his wife and I stood there for a second, then his wife burst into laughter! She said to her husband, "You finally found someone that likes to haggle as much as you do!" He paused for a second and then laughed and said, "OK!" It was a great job.

All other times, though, I never back up on a bid. People may try to shame you, intimidate you, or get angry with you to get you to lower the price. But resist. If you give in, especially out of fear of losing the job, and do the job for a lower price, they will be on your case most times all the way through the job. This is not just my experience. I have talked to others that have experienced the exact same thing. Why? Because they see that you have no respect for yourself, and then they don't respect you either. But they will take the lower price.

I bid a job once, and the man said, "When contractors see a Nichols Hills address, they get dollars signs in their eyes. The last guy did it for half this much." I said, "Get him to do it." In the end I got the job after I told him to call the store and get some more bids. Our bid was right in line. His wife later told me that they did not like the quality of the previous workman. So they were trying to get a better contractor for the same price as the one that did the shoddy work. They will lie and be deceitful as well to get you to lower your price. I got the job at the original bid price and had no trouble with the job. Stick up for yourself. People can smell confidence, and it sells.

People can also smell insecurity or fear of loss like a dog smells fear. They don't consciously think about it, but they know and they act on your lack of confidence and belief in yourself.

Backing up on a bid does several things:

> First, it damages your self-image, your self-confidence, and your sense of worthiness.

> You have to protect your sense of self-worth, or you will allow people to walk on you all your life. You have to protect your self-image and your self-confidence. This is very important. Remember, there is a great difference between arrogance and confidence. We are quietly confident but not arrogant.

> Second, the customer/client realizes that you are not confident in yourself, your business, or your ability.

> They may feel that you were willing to accept a lower price because you needed the work. If you need the work, then how good are you really? The client/customer will think to themselves, "I better keep an eye on this one if they do the job because they are probably not very good if they need the work that bad."

> Once you accept the idea of backing up on a bid/price, you will do it again and again. Then you will begin to bid your jobs or

products lower still. This is where the practice of upping the bid by 10% is a good habit.

They may constantly push you to do more than what was contracted for. When they pushed on the price, you caved, so they are hoping you will cave more.

Many contractors falsely believe that most people make their choice of contractors based on mostly price. In one of the surveys I read years ago, price came in fifth in the order of consideration by people accepting bids. Many other things are more important to people than price.

Even if you are new in your field, you need to price yourself right at the market price; no exceptions.

Even if people have not heard of you before in your field, they will instantly recognize that you must be good, and that you have some confidence in your ability and in your products. That is the reputation that you want to instill from the very outset.

Now if the service or products normally sell for $20.00, you cannot price it at $50.00, or you will go broke. But pricing it at $10.00 is a great mistake.

Usually prices are set by the free market because that is the price where the vendor can sell his service or product and make a reasonable profit. And everyone knows what that price point is. So you stick out like a sore thumb when you come in low.

If you do not know at what price to bid the job/product, start with a reasonable price. If you get every job, you are priced too low. The way I see it is that if you lose 20% of the bids you make, you are probably right in line with what the market is willing to pay. If the calls are cold, in other words from the yellow pages or a website, I would expect to get only about 20% of those jobs anyway. Most of those people are just shopping prices, and there is always a low baller out there. You are not in competition with the low ballers.

I bid a job over the phone one night, and the lady said that another service said they would do the job for $150.00. That was $200.00 lower than my price. I told her I understood, but that the people that give bids like that are generally involved with apartments, do no prep work to make sure it is a good job, and that if the job fails, they charge another $150.00 to do it over. I told her we do not compete in that market. She said, "That is what I kind of thought. Come do my job." Confidence sells along with asking God for the right words.

If you will go with the market price from the beginning, you will be accepted as a viable source from the outset if you or your product perform the way it should.

Finally, if you back up on a bid or bid the job less than the market, you will get a reputation that, "If you push him, he will come down." What does that say about you, your ability, your business, your work-manship, your confidence and your self-image? Is that the reputation/self-image that you want? NO! Be confident. It will pay off well.

If you back up on a bid or bid the job less than the market that is not fair to you. The laborer is worthy of his hire, and it is not fair to your family. You and your family deserve to be paid well for your work. You deserve to be paid just as well as the other guy. And you will find at times that some older businesses have not kept their pricing up to date. Do not let that discourage you from keeping your prices up.

One of the hardest things to see and remember is that your price is not just for the labor. How much did it cost you to set your business up? How much time did you invest in yourself to learn to do what you do? Remember, that you are a business not just a day laborer. The plumbing company charges $125.00 per hour to cover their costs and to pay the plumber. They pay the plumber, the laborer, about $15.00 per hour. **You are a business not a laborer.**

They are paying for your knowledge and your ability to solve problems.

There are always exceptions to the rule but very rarely. Maybe once in five years!

Sometimes you can set the market price yourself. One area I was involved in a few years ago, the job was currently priced at $350.00. I was told a couple of years later by someone who knew that the price had dropped to about $150.00. It was true as I asked people what the other bids were when there were some other bids. I decided to set the standard for the pricing and kept our price at $350.00. Within a couple of years, the price was back up and then went even higher. Have some respect for yourself and your ability.

I have at times given a cheaper price to an elderly person. Not often, but once in a while when "the spirit moves me."

I remember a story told to me by a banker in a small town years ago that I was working for. She said that when the town finally put in a city sewer line, all the residents were required to pay their share. But there was one elderly lady that lived in a tumble down house on the edge of town that sold vegetables from her garden on the street in the summer time. The town council voted to put her sewer in at no charge. The banker said that she could not tell them, but that lady had several million dollars in the bank in CD's. Things are not always as they seem!

Remember, price yourself at the market from the beginning. It may be a little scary, but you will see the benefits if you will do it. Then once you have given a price, stick with it.

Proverbs 14:33 Wisdom is enshrined in an understanding heart....
(New Living Translation)

"Become a sponge for information that will help you on your way. You don't have to waste years making the mistakes others have made before." Earl Nightingale

CHAPTER 4

Don't Divide Out a Bid

Rule #5 – Never Do Time and Materials.

Whenever possible, do not do time and materials. It is much more profitable to do a flat bid for a specific amount of work. For instance, let's say you bid a certain amount of work at $225.00, and it takes you two hours to complete. If you bill them time of 2 hours @ $100.00 each and materials for $25.00, they will probably balk at that. No one wants to pay $100.00/hour for labor. But they will not hesitate to pay the $225.00 for a bid job most of the time.

I realize some jobs have to be time and materials. Many painters bid large jobs that way. Just make sure you are paid well for what you do.

A key here is this: The longer the job, the more hours, the less you will likely earn per hour. Although long jobs have a sense of job security that comes with them many times, many small jobs bid properly can produce a better income.

Rule #6 – Avoid an Expanding Scope of Work.

People will try to add things on at the last minute like adding another room or doing some necessary repairs along with what you have already bid to do. They figure that you have that time set aside and rather than risk not working, you will do more for free because you will fear losing the job. Many see contractors as being broke, begging for work and unable to feed and clothe their families.

We simply reiterate what we are doing and the price. Then we say, "If you need more done, I can price that to you now. Then you can decide before I get started, or before I come back tomorrow if you want the additional work done." Stick up for yourself.

Once you stand up for yourself, that type of adding on usually stops, and it also makes them realize that you have a backbone and won't be pushed. That can save you grief in other areas of the job as well.

Rule #7 – Don't Divide out a Bid.

In bidding a job, it works well to see what the customer wants done, then call them back later with a price. After you think about it for a while in a relaxed frame of mind, you will remember to add in things that you may have overlooked or forgotten if you bid it right on the spot.

Sometimes when you come back with a price, the customer will ask if you can divide out the bid for him. They may say how about if we left this off, then what would you charge. Once they have the list of prices then they will say, "Well, my buddy Bob was going to do the prep work, so could you take that out also?" Then they think they can buy the materials cheaper than what you are charging.

First, we quit doing jobs where someone else does the prep work a long time ago. Those never work out well. If the prep work was not done properly they will say, "Hey, I already paid to have it done once, you will just have to deal with what they did." Now you either walk away or redo the prep work at your cost with no pay.

If the customer was going to buy the materials, cut out a room, and have Bob do the prep work, the honest thing would have been for them to tell you that up front. If you are only going to end up doing a small part of the original work, you would have probably bid it higher than if it is included in a larger project. IF YOU WERE TO BREAK the bid down, each part should be substantially higher in cost!

If they buy the materials, they may not buy what you are used to working with, but they will expect you to stand behind the work even if the materials are inferior. And they may not buy ALL the materials necessary but expect you to fill in the blanks at your cost.

You should be marking up your materials, too, by the way. There is time in buying and transporting, and you are in a way financing part of the job until the materials are paid for unless they pay for the materials up front.

Once you have given them a bid, stick with that bid. People that want the bid divided out generally are going to be trouble all the way through the job.

I have had people ask, "How long will that take you, and what are your costs?" They want to know the price per hour they are paying, or to see if they can do the easy part and get you to lower your price on the harder stuff. No! You just respond with the quoted price. We do not break down the costs for anyone. We may take into account what we need to make per hour and our costs per job, but the quote is a flat price. Be firm but not mean. Remember, it is a business and with the right attitude about your business and yourself, it will build respect with your clients.

You will see these things come up as you work. Just remember the principles. The more you abide by them the better your outcomes will be.

Be prepared to walk away instead of giving in to their demands. Many times I have been called back to do the work after I stuck to my guns in pricing. But I had no more trouble during the job.

People will push you to see if there is any give in you. If there is give in you, they will push on everything in the job.

So these principles have a common denominator. Have a backbone; stand up for yourself. Decide how you are going to structure your business and stick with it. It will pay great dividends going down the road.

Rule #8 – Never Downgrade Your Competition.

Always admit that they are good, that they are just an alternative to you.

If you have ever listened to someone downgrade their competitors, it gives a terrible impression of the one talking. It is so easy to see that they are trying to look better by belittling others. That never works. People know what you are doing and why. You will seem like a small begrudging person.

You will gain a much greater reputation by being polite about your competition.

I know there are many of these rules. But if you read them frequently and then talk to other good, older contractors about them, you will find most have learned these same rules the way I did -- the hard way by experience. They just never bothered to number the rules and write them down.

Rule #9 – Don't Work for Friends.

Working for friends can be a great way to end a friendship. There is an old saying that "familiarity breeds contempt." They often feel like you should do it much cheaper for them since they know you, but they will expect you to deliver the moon. If you discount the work to them, they will still want more discounts on everything. The bigger the job the more they will want.

The only way to avoid these problems in contracting that I know of is to tell your friend up front what you are willing to do on price.

Then tell them up front how you run your business. Any changes will come with a changes estimate and have to be paid in cash up front. You have to stick strictly to your policies even though they are your friends. Once they see you will not budge, I suspect they will leave you alone.

I once knew a builder whose client wanted to change the can lights after they were installed. He gave them a price and the customer said, "I don't want to have the hassle of this over every change. Just bring the bills to the closing, and I will pay for them then." The builder took $60,000.00 worth of change orders to the closing. The customer then said, "I am not paying for that. This is a custom home; you should have calculated those changes into the price." That builder ate the money.

Stick to your principles. If I were the builder, I would have refused to close and would have put the house on the market as a spec house and would have taken the loss selling their home to someone else.

Rule #10 – Verify /

We verify everything. We verify addresses, who is paying, and that they are home now so we can come over. I had a builder that set up an appointment once and would not give us the homeowner's number. I got there at the set time and no one was home. I called the builder and asked her when she verified they would be there. Three days earlier! I left. This is why we require the phone number of the person that is going to meet us there.

Many times a husband will say, "My wife will be there all day; just go on over." "Can I get her phone number?" "Sure." When I call, she says, "I am not at home. I have a dentist appointment, then a Junior

League meeting, and then I have to pick the kids up from school. I don't know why he says those things without checking with me first." --- Verify!

Proverbs 11:12 He who belittles and despises his neighbor lacks sense, but a man of understanding keeps silent (Amplified Bible)

There are three things that are important to every man in this locker room. His God, his family and the Green Bay Packers. In that order. Vince Lombardi

CHAPTER 5

Keep Your Integrity!

When I first got into this business, my focus was on solving the problems of the people that called. I would say, "No problem," and get it fixed ASAP.

But as time went on and I became very busy, I began to try to get them to wait on me by getting them to sympathize with my problems in getting there in a timely fashion. I talked about too many of the things going on in my life that were negative.

As I was talking one day, I could tell by the man's face that he really did not want to hear all that. As I thought about what I was doing, I realized that my focus had dramatically changed from being a problem solver to being a problem teller.

People are looking for problem solvers. They're not concerned with your problems. They just want their problems fixed. If you have too many problems, they will find somebody who doesn't have so many.

So that's how **Rule #11** came about.

Rule #11 – Don't tell people about your problems!

Your business will do better!

Rule #12 – Never work for just one company or client.

My sons were in Boy Scouts a number of years ago, and the Scout Master at the time was an attorney. He had worked for the same company for about 20 years and had no private practice. He had a nice home and a son in college, but when the oil company made some cuts, he was out of a job. Since he had never developed a private practice, he was in bad shape. He finally went to work for another attorney in the troop that had his own law firm.

It is never good as a contractor to only work for one company or client. They can really put your feet to the fire at times to get lower prices – their own houses done cheaply or their jobs done for free.

I worked for an acquaintance one time that had just had a new home built by a large builder. She told me that all the contractors on her home told her that they had just built their foreman a new home with free labor. They either did his home for free or found another job. What could they do? He was their only client.

I have been offered large jobs in the past that may take a year or so. First, they want it done at a cheaper price because of the volume of the work and the job security it offers. Then they want to be your only client. I have always turned those deals down. What happens at the end of the work? I would have no business left to go back to. All my clients will have found other contractors, and I will have to start from scratch building a business.

They may decide in six months they want the price even cheaper. They have you over a barrel. They are your only source of income.

What if they decide in six months that Bob can do it even cheaper? They will drop you in a heartbeat.

Trading your freedom of running your own business for the security of work every day is not worth the risk.

Rule #13 – Don't stir the pot.

This can cover many different areas.

I used to tell builders things that I saw wrong with their houses that might cause them trouble down the road. I found they usually took that as criticism. Now I will tell them if the house is on fire, but that is about it.

I used to try to help people get their jobs done under the warranty they had. That required many phone calls to set it up. I found that the some of the people I had to contact in order to accomplish this did not appreciate it. As we could not turn in the warranty job ourselves, it required several calls to find out if the responsible entity had turned the job in for the people. I quit stirring the warranty pot also.

Not stirring the pot is a good principle to live by in your work and in everyday life. The more you ponder it and watch, the better you will understand.

Rule #14 – Keep how much you make to yourself.

This is a great rule. Each business has its own list of expenses and financial duties and benefits that most outside that business will not understand.

Years ago my mother saw a milk check (proceeds from a dairy farm for the milk they sold that week) that came into my aunt's books. Mother said, "Boy, I would like to have that for a week." My aunt said, "It looks like a lot, but if you saw the bills I have to pay, it would not seem like very much."

People will not understand how your business is set up and perhaps what all is involved in the price you set. So it is best to just keep what you make to yourself.

Rule #15 – Keep Your Integrity.

Integrity is one of the most valuable assets you can have as a business person. Integrity says you can be trusted: trusted to tell the truth in situations – trusted to do what is right.

But integrity is often sacrificed on the altar of money.

I have a book that I look at often that has things I pray about in it. At the top of the page is a list of priorities for life that I learned from Jim Rohn (a self-development speaker). It is a very good way of ordering the priorities of your life.

1. God
2. Health
3. Family
4. Integrity
5. Career

Many people put their career in the number one position. That would have to do with the making of money. If you do this, you will sacrifice your relationship with God, your health, your relationship with your family and your integrity for the sake of your career or in other words, money.

God should always come first. Then should come the taking care of your health. Without health you are no good to your family or your career.

Family should come next and always before your career. Then comes your integrity. If you sacrifice your integrity for the sake of your career, you may lose your career also.

You may be tempted to lie to benefit a builder or plumber, etc. But once they know you lie, can they ever really rely on your telling the truth in any other situation? If they really need an honest assessment, they will have to ask someone else. Because they know you cannot be trusted.

I have lost accounts and friends because I would not change the facts to benefit them. But if that is what they required for them to be my friend or for me to keep their business, is that what I want to build my life on? My answer is always the same. NO. Keep your integrity. It is worth far more than money or position or more jobs.

I was analyzing a job for a hotel one time and told them what they should do. One partner said to the other, "They told me you may not like what he tells you, but he will tell you the truth." That is the reputation that you want.

In the long haul, having great integrity and being a person that can be trusted will pay great dividends. Always Keep Your Integrity.

Proverbs 17:24 Wisdom is the main pursuit of sensible men..... (The Living Bible)

Work hard at your job, and you can make a living.
Work hard on yourself, and you can make a fortune. Jim Rohn

CHAPTER 6

Have Some Respect

Rule #16 – Have Some Respect for Yourself

It would seem that there are many things to learn when you are learning about The Prosperous Life.

First, you would want to get born from above. No matter how much money you make or how high you climb in the corporate world or politics, if all you have to look forward to is 70 years and a hole in the ground; that is not much of a prosperous life.

If you have confessed Jesus Christ as your Lord and if you believe that God raised him from the dead, then you truly already have a prosperous eternal life to look forward to.

While we are awaiting the return of our lord, there are many aspects to The Prosperous Life to learn about. This one aspect starts with a story.

I walked into a warehouse the other day that I am in occasionally and observed the people walking around and through. There were people from the office, dressed very nicely, passing through checking on orders, men who apparently had decided that the warehouse was their life's work, and another man that was the warehouse manager.

The warehouse manager was dressed nicely as well, clean shaven, nice work pants, shirt tucked in and smiling as he hurried about.

The other people who probably were going to be warehousemen for the rest of their lives dressed less thoughtfully. Their pants needed washing. Their shirts were not tucked in. Some needed to shave.

It was easy to tell which ones were heading up. The next stop would be counter sales and then outside sales which would all pay better than working in the warehouse.

A few years ago, I was with a man that was doing bathtub repairs for a living. He got a speck of paint on his jeans and it irritated him. He said, "Today was the last day for these jeans as they are threadbare, and I got paint on them. Darn!" He took pride in keeping his clothes clean from paint until they were worn out. It was like a self-imposed challenge to keep his clothes spotless.

On the other hand, I have seen many painters that are covered in paint wearing clothes that look like they have not been washed in a month. They wear those paint covered clothes like a badge of honor. "I am a painter!!" constantly wiping their paint covered hands on their pants.

How much work would it be to keep a towel on your belt to wipe your hands on and keep your clothes clean?

I have a paint store that I have bought supplies from for years. I have seen the owner many times in the back mixing paint with never a spot on his clothes. His wife buys his shirts from garage sales cheap, and when he gets paint on one, it goes in the trash. He is always neat. He cares about his appearance, and he will probably take care to get your order right.

In the work I do, I am constantly knocking on people's doors during the daytime. Many times the husband is at work and when that young woman with two young ones in tow looks out the peep hole, what do you think she would be more comfortable seeing? Someone dressed neatly, and clean shaven or someone with grease and paint on their pants, holes in their shirt, and a three day old beard on their face?

A three day beard on Friday night may be cool, but it is not cool when knocking on a young woman's door, whose husband is gone, on Monday morning. It looks scraggily!

This is not just my thinking. Some of the companies that I work for call the people after we have fixed the issue in their customer's home. They ask the client:

- Were they on time?
- Were they dressed nicely?
- Were they clean shaven?
- Were you comfortable with them in your home?"

The reason is because I may be the only person associated with that company that the client has ever seen, and the company wants to be represented well.

How you dress says a lot about you. If you don't pay much attention to how you dress, maybe you are not going to:

- Pay much attention to your job,
- Or to your speech,
- Or to the important details of your companies clients,
- Or their orders.

Sometimes people will try you out on a job or two to see what you are like -- how do you dress, do you show up on time, are you easy to work with, etc. If they like what they see, you could step into a mega account. You just never know where the next job will lead. This is why establishing good work ethics, principles and habits will pay off in the long run.

One painting company I was on a forum with on the internet said this: "When our guys come to work, they are expected to wear clean clothes and if they have not shaved, I tell them that there are razors and shaving cream in the restroom. They either shave or they go home."

I have read about painters that run large shops, and sometimes they include paperhanging as part of their services. One paint company owner said he had two good paperhangers. One was a young guy that did absolutely superb work and an old man whose work was good but certainly not the quality of the younger man. Now the young man was a sloppy dresser, kind of slovenly in appearance. The older man dressed in traditional painter/paperhanger clothes -- slacks, dress shoes, white shirt and tie. When the painter came to work dressed like this, they would put on some overalls AFTER they had met the people of the home for the day and the owners had gone to work. When the clients would call back to the shop to request more paper to be hung guess which paperhanger had the most requests? The old man!! I have heard of this happening in several cases. Sloppy personal habits make people uneasy. The workers seem less trustworthy. Sloppy appearance and work habits are irritating to some people and others are not quite sure they want to leave the person home alone or with their children.

How you dress, personal hygiene, etc. says a lot about how you think about your job and yourself and your ability. This may not be true for every person, **but it is what goes through the minds of the people that have the ability to promote you or hire you.**

You could learn to observe how the people above you in the company dress and copy their style. (Unless they are slobs!) You will move up faster. (It should go without saying, but sometimes needs to be said anyway, take a bath and use some deodorant!)

Some people seem to think that once they are hired for a job, it is theirs for life and how they conduct themselves and how they dress is irrelevant. Your boss may never tell you what he thinks about how you take care of yourself, but, if you don't pay attention to your outward appearance, don't be surprised if you are passed up for promotions. Have some respect for yourself.

Everywhere we go we represent our Father and the company that sent us. This is simply another piece of The Prosperous Life.

Proverbs 22:1 A good name is to be chosen rather than great riches....
(The Living Bible)

CHAPTER 7

Comfortable and Complacent!

Rule #17 – Don't Become Comfortable and Complacent!

I meet many people every day, and many times I ask them what they do for work and/or how they got into the business they are in. Sometimes the stories are very interesting. I asked a young builder the other day how he came to build houses.

He said he was working as a foreman for another builder making about $50,000 per year. He told me that it is very easy to become complacent with that kind of income. He said you can pay your bills and live fairly comfortably.

Together he and his wife had read many financial books and had some understanding of how money worked. He said he did not want to become complacent at that level of income, so after he learned what he felt he needed to know about building houses, after about a year with this job, he quit.

He found a money man that agreed to build seven houses and split the profits 50/50 with him, and that venture was successful. A year later they parted company, and he now had enough to go the bank. They loaned him the money to start a couple of houses, and he was in the building business.

Many times we become complacent with our income because we are comfortable there.

- We know what it takes to earn that amount.
- We know the people.
- We know the routines.
- We know that we can pay our bills at that level.
- Our friends all make about the same.
- We are part of the group.

If we strive to move up a level or two, that would put us in unfamiliar territory. Weird as it sounds, most people would be uncomfortable if their income doubled or tripled.

- Their lifestyle might change.
- Their friends might change.
- What they talk about might change.
- And most are afraid of the unknown.

You see many people have bought into the idea that to really be successful you have to get a college education and go to work for some major company. That can be very comfortable – someone or a company taking care of you, and then complacency can easily set in. You could fight complacency, and climb out of your comfort zone.

Starting your own side business may be uncomfortable and may be a little different than your friends, but it may change your life in ways you never imagined.

For example: I have met people that buy and sell golf courses or others that buy companies from the IRS that were taken because of non-payment of taxes. They got the companies profitable and then sold them. I have also talked to people that buy mobile home parks after the park had been through bankruptcy two or three times. Then they made a deal with a company that repossessed mobile homes to put them in their park and split the rent.

Some 150 years ago most of the people in this country were self-employed as we were an agricultural economy. But as the industrial age set in, people moved from the farms into the cities. Then they acquired some debt and had to stay in those jobs in order to pay "the man." But it was comfortable. A paycheck each week. Eventually complacency can set in.

This reminds one of the song *Sixteen Tons* by Tennessee Ernie Ford. One of the lines reads: "Saint Peter don't you call 'cause I can't go, I owe my soul to the company store."

This lack of funds and debt keeps us showing up on the job to get the money to pay the debt. We have been trained to be good workers for industry and good consumers for the global economy. **Someone sold us on the wrong plan.**

A billboard I see every day says: "A job for every Oklahoman, a work-force for every company." Learn to think outside the box.

Learn to embrace the uncomfortable and beware of complacency. God wants us to be God-sufficient. For God to be our sufficiency, a college education is not required. God's hand is with us in everything we do as we are His children. So break out of your comfort zone, and kiss complacency goodbye. God has laid out the fundamental principles of prosperity in His Word. These fundamental principles are also laid out in our new book *Poverty vs Wealth*. Try it. It could be your key to The Prosperous Life.

Proverbs 24:10 If you faint in the day of adversity your strength is small.
(English Standard Version)

CHAPTER 8

Staying Out of Trouble

Someone once said that we don't communicate well enough. There may be many reasons for that: the wrong choice of words, being unclear about what we really mean, or because we are trying to imply something we hope the person gets, but we really don't want to come right out and say it.

By rephrasing the words back to the speaker, we can verify that what we are hearing is what the speaker meant. This can be done with your spouse, children, coworkers or even your boss.

Rephrasing is to say back to the person, in your own words, what they said. "What I hear you saying is….."

Example:

"What's for dinner?"

"We were going to have chicken, but I forgot to thaw it out, and I have been so busy today I hadn't even thought about it."

"So are you wanting to go out for supper?"

"Would you mind?"

Here is another example: The salesman writes up a repair order on two of his products sitting in a wholesaler's warehouse. His company sends the repair order to an independent repair contractor. The contractor sees that one unit is a warranty repair and one has been damaged, probably by the wholesaler's warehousemen. The repairman calls the manufacturer, and the manufacturer agrees to pay for the one unit with the defect but refuses to pay for the other damaged one.

During the repair the salesman shows up and says to the repairman.

"You are new at this aren't you? I would hate to lose an account like this as I only have two accounts. Don't let little "technicalities" cause us to lose this account. This time I will pay for the non-warranty repair."

Rephrasing: "So what I hear you saying is that no matter what is wrong with the units, you want me to write up the invoice to the manufacturer to show that these are all warranty repairs. Is that right?"

If he says, "yes," now you know he wants you to lie. You can:

1. Just end the conversation without confirming that you will do that and next time it happens, mention to the manufacturer what you have been instructed to do by their salesman.
2. Let him know that you will only bill warranty repairs to the manufacturer, and if he wants to pay for all the others, you will call him each time to confirm his continued willingness to pay.

Rule #18 – Practice Rephrasing Anything Questionable or Unclear.

Rephrasing can clear up many situations. It can help straighten out fuzzy thinking, help use the right words, make things clearer and at times keep you out of trouble.

Communicating well is part of The Prosperous Life.

Rule #19 – Never Look in the Windows.

I learned this from a direct sales company 45 years ago and have followed it ever since. If you look in the windows of the house you are knocking on, first of all to passersby or even the homeowner, you appear to be a rube (an uneducated, unsophisticated country boy). This is just rude.

What if you arrived a little earlier that the lady had anticipated, and you see her racing half-dressed to the other end of the house and she sees you? No matter what you do, that situation is a mess. And remember people talk.

I first ring the doorbell then turn away slightly from the door and step back a bit if that is possible. On the second ring if the door is not answered, I also add a knock. Sometimes doorbells don't work. Then we try a third time before I would call them on the phone. Sometimes they are running the vacuum, etc. and did not hear you.

If you stand back a ways, you don't seem to be so much in their space when they open the door.

Think about it!

Proverbs15:8.... The prayers of the upright are his delight (The New KJV)

*Move out of your comfort zone. You can only grow if you are willing to feel
awkward and uncomfortable when you try something new. Brian Tracy*

CHAPTER 9

Be Bold!

Rule #20 – Be Bold When It Comes to Money

Fear stops us from living a truly prosperous life at times. I have been in contracting for about 40 years, and in that time I have seen many people lose money and go broke because of the fear of asking to get paid. Boldness is far better and more profitable than fear.

You don't have to be rude. Just ask. Or in some cases let them know that you need to be paid when the job is complete. We always do this on commercial jobs.

As we conclude the phone conversation about time and pricing, I just tell them we need to get paid the day we are done. They may say they don't carry checks. We ask if they have a credit card and then ask if that will work for their boss. Also we add $3.50/hundred to do a card because that is what we are charged. Most of the time, they agree.

That is so much simpler than trying to collect from a company that is out of state. If you have ever tried that kind of collecting, you will know what I mean. Generally, it takes three months to get money that way. We just don't do jobs like that anymore.

With smaller, local contractors we usually ask them to meet us and pay when we are done when it is the first time we have worked for them. Usually, people understand the situation and do just what you ask. If that goes well, we will bill them in the future.

If they object, then that raises a red flag. They may be ones that you would have a hard time collecting from anyway. Tell them you really need to get paid while you are there because they are a new account.

If you stick to your guns, usually they will do that.

This type of dealing with people about money also has the advantage of showing that:

1. You have some integrity.
2. You are not afraid of losing a job.
3. You respect yourself enough to conduct your business properly.
4. Thus, most people will have more respect for you and treat you better.

I worked with a young man years ago that told me the builder owed him for all the materials and labor for five houses. WOW! I asked him why he would do the next one if he was not getting paid.

Fear was the answer:

1. Afraid the builder would not pay for any of it if he asked for the money.
2. Afraid he would not get the next job if he insisted on getting paid.
3. Afraid of the confrontation.

He eventually went broke and got a job.

Fear... some call it sand in the machinery of life.

(More on this in **Rule #45**)

Boldness without being rude is one of the well-worn paths to The Prosperous Life.

Proverbs 28:1 .... But the righteous are bold as a lion (KJV)

Once you learn to quit, it becomes a habit. Vince Lombardi

CHAPTER 10

How to Make Yourself Heard

Rule #21 - Learn Good Marketing Skills

When I first went into business for myself, my first client said, "I already have a service provider, but they won't answer the phone, and they won't call me back." So that became my first rule: Always call them back; always be available. One thing I've learned, people will accept a lower standard of quality if you are easily available. Not returning phone calls is very frustrating to people no matter how great your quality of services or products are. If they are in a hurry, if they need it done right now, and they know they can get a hold of you, they will call you even if your quality is not as good as the other guys. This is not an excuse for poor quality, but just to show how important good marketing is. Being available by phone is part of marketing.

You don't have to be the best in your field to be successful, but you do have to know about marketing. Marketing can include many different things:

- the way you dress,
- phone call etiquette,
- business cards,
- websites, etc.,
- AND knowing who holds the key in your market.

One of my accounts told me that they used our quick responses to phone calls and service calls to sell their products because the other service provider at times took months to get the jobs done. So we use our fast response to phone calls as part of our marketing. We put on our business cards, "We return telephone calls promptly." That wholesaler used us to market their products.

Marketing does not have to cost a lot of money. I like the principles of Guerilla Marketing which is low cost or no cost marketing. It is very effective even though it might be free. One of the best authors on the subject is J. Abrams. He is great at Guerilla Marketing and has written several books on the topic. Getting Everything You Can Out of All You've Got: 21 Ways You Can Out-Think, Out-Perform, and Out-Earn the Competition is one of his well-known books.

Sometimes all it takes is one or two good ideas to make a huge difference in your marketing.

I remember reading in one of Robert Kyosaki's books a conversation he had with a young female writer. He said, "I have read your work and you are very good." "Yes," she responded, "but I don't sell very many books." Robert said, "You need to look into marketing." She responded, "I am a college grad, and that would be 'sales'!" (Sales are a little beneath the class of a college grad). Robert told her he was not nearly as good a writer as she was, but he sold a lot of books. He said that marketing is the key. You don't have to be the best at your craft, but if you can market well, that will put you right up at the top.

If you have days or a week or two when you are not busy (as we all do if we run a small business or are self-employed), one thing to know is that you will get busy again. So, in those off times, that's when you can concentrate on marketing. You can:

- Work on your website or websites.
- Work on your twitter accounts.
- Clean out your truck.
- Organize your materials.
- Post to Facebook.

- Post to Instagram.
- Work on expediting your processes.
- Talk to your mentors.
- Talk to the key pins in your marketing process such as wholesalers, manufacturers, or large clients.
- Read books on marketing.
- Strategize.

In order for people to beat a path to your door, they have to know about you. Every field requires a different marketing strategy. Marketing can also include branding, a logo, and/or twitter accounts. If you are marketing a book, Michael Hyatt's book, Platform: Get Noticed in a Noisy World is helpful.

Another book is Jeff Walker's book: *Launch: An Internet Millionaire's Secret Formula To Sell Almost Anything Online, Build A Business You Love, And Live The Life Of Your Dreams.*

Probably the biggest key is to pray a lot. God's hand is with you because you are one of His children, and you should expect to see His hand at work to open doors for your business and to protect your business.

The Bible says that wisdom is worth more than rubies. Marketing is a type of wisdom. Once you learn the importance of it and the rudiments of how to do it, it can make you a lot of money. Without marketing, you could have the greatest service, product or book in the world and be very short on sales.

I have asked many people what they do to market their business. Many times their response is, "My work speaks for itself, and I get most of my work or business through referrals." I believe this is a lazy man's way of saying he is content with what he gets even if it is not much.

Marketing works. If all that was required was word of mouth, why do so many businesses advertise?

Walmart, Kohl's, Stihl, movies, drug companies, Ford Motor Company, and the list goes on forever. It is because marketing works.

Many people are very good at what they do, like the female writer above, but they never really reach their full monetary potential because of a lack of understanding of marketing. We want to not only be good in our craft, business or books but good at marketing, too. That gives us a full package for a prosperous venture in our living The Prosperous Life.

Proverbs 21:5 Good planning and hard work lead to prosperity, but hasty shortcuts lead to poverty. New Living Translation

You don't get paid for the hour. You get paid for the value you bring to the hour. Jim Rohn

Charge Like a Business

Rule #22 – Charge Like a Business

The lady says, "You don't charge for that do you? You just got here." Sometimes our job only takes one to five minutes.

The builder standing there watching says, "That did not take long. Are you giving me a discounted price?"

Another lady says, "Wow! That was simple. I'll bet you don't charge the builder much do you?"

"It is a trip charge ma'am."

"I am going to turn you in to the builder!"

A new contractor told me one time that they only charge $15-20/ hour.

One thing all these people have in common is that they are thinking in terms of paying a labor charge.

Think about it. There is a great difference between paying a business for coming to your home and paying a day laborer you have hired to work. One is a business – and one is a laborer.

If an electrician comes to your house and all he has to do is change out a light bulb to fix the problem, you still pay his company's minimum trip charge because he represents and works for a business.

Most businesses should have a minimum trip charge for work, inspections on site, or giving advice on site. For example, in contracting these trip charges may run from $95.00 to $150.00. The business charges the trip charge, and they pay the electrician or plumber by the hour for their labor, $15-25.00 per hour.

The expenses to run a business are much greater than the expenses of showing up to work as a laborer.

I have listed here some of the expenses a business has to pay for overhead.

Expenses for a business:

- Workman's Comp Insurance
- Contractor's Liability Insurance
- Local Licenses
- Truck
- Truck Insurance
- Fuel
- Vehicle Maintenance
- Fax Machine/Printer/Copier
- Land Line for Phone
- Cell Phone
- Computer
- Bookkeeping Software
- Other Types of Software
- Internet Access
- Office Space
- Office Equipment
- Office Supplies
- Tools and Equipment

- Supplies
- Website
- Website Design and Management
- Drive time to the job

Expenses for laborer:

- Clothes
- Shoes

So if you are just beginning the business of contracting and you have been a laborer for years, you have to change how you think. It may be a shock to your mind to now charge like a business instead of being paid for labor, but you can do it. Many other people have made the jump.

Since you are a business and not just a worker or laborer, you may need to dress like you own a business. Think like a business man or woman, and see yourself as one who owns a business.

You cannot charge $15-20 per hour, pay the list of expenses itemized above, then hand your spouse the change and expect them to pay all your personal household expenses. You will go broke.

If you are going to contract business, you have to charge like a business!

Proverbs 13:11 Wealth from get-rich-quick schemes quickly disappears; wealth from hard work grows over time. New Living Translation

C H A P T E R   1 2

Hoping To Get Paid!

I f you take a job "hoping" to get paid, several things happen.

Just like a dog can smell fear, people can "smell" that attitude in the contractor.

It communicates that:

1. You don't have much confidence in yourself or your ability.
2. You are not a real business.
3. You come off as a low status contractor or business.
4. When you give away your expertise and/or your knowledge for free, that is the poor contractor mentality. It is also why so many contractors are poor. They don't really think much of themselves or the service they provide.

Rule #23 – We Never Do A Job Hoping To Get Paid.

But that is not the only problem. The real problem is what happens in your mind.

Think about how you feel each time you take a job or look at a job "hoping" to get paid. At the least, it is demeaning. You feel terrible on the inside and at the mercy of the person.

I sent a text to another contractor today that stated: "They are hiring you or buying your services to see if the unit can be saved. Whether the repair of the unit looks acceptable or not, they have still hired you. Don't do **<u>anything</u>** for free hoping to make a little money. That damages your psyche."

Some people, knowing how you feel, or how you see yourself, will use that against you. "Well, that is not quite what I expected. I was expecting something a little better." Now you feel guilty for asking to be paid. Many times things cannot be made perfect.

There are much better ways of dealing with these situations.

You have to have enough respect for yourself to **believe** and **know** that you deserve to be paid. That attitude has quite a different "smell," and most people can tell that one, too.

I had a builder call today and ask me to look at a certain problem he had and let him know if it could be repaired. I told him he might as well let me repair it while I was there because the cost was the same for a trip charge to "look" as it was to repair. Once it was repaired, then he could decide if he wanted to keep the unit or replace it. He agreed to that idea. I will get paid even if he replaces the unit.

By handling the situation this way, he knows he will have to pay for my services either way. It feels much better for me also. It is fair to him and also to me and my family. Rather than doing this inspection for free, I could be doing another job that paid.

People should expect to pay you. They are paying for your expertise and knowledge. Folks should expect to pay for that. We have many calls where they just want us to "come take a look" at their problem, whatever it is. We are upfront and tell them it is $XX.XX for us to "look". Knowing that we have a service fee for looking at a problem, many are glad to pay it.

So I recommend they send us pictures, and we can go from there. Since we do charge for inspections, we try to solve problems over the phone from pictures and give those recommendations for free. Once I explain why we need the pictures, that we are trying to save them the cost of an inspection, they are usually grateful.

If people in your area learn you are willing to come "take a look" for free, you will not have time to make a living. They will bury you in calls.

When you tell clients up front what you charge for your services, generally, they are willing to pay that -- especially if you come recommended.

If you don't bring up the cost of an inspection until you tell them it cannot be repaired, they many times will balk at paying you. They will say you did not do anything.

It is not fair or honest for people to expect you to give away your recommendations for free if you have to visit their job site. It is also not fair or honest to have you attempt to do a job they know may not be perfect and then expect not to pay. With inspections, sometimes that is unavoidable especially if it is for a large client. But even with them, you can be frank and let them know what your fee is for inspections, recommendations or advice. Remember, they are **hiring** you to attempt to repair or to recommend.

It is also not fair to your family to give away for free what has taken you years to acquire in knowledge and expertise. Your family deserves better than "free."

You will also be able to hold your head a little higher, people will have much more respect for you and they will have more respect for your recommendations and attempts to make a bad unit acceptable. This feels far better than "hoping" to get paid. It is a completely different attitude.

This is not done with any arrogance or haughty pride but just with an expectation of being paid for your service whether it is an inspection or an actual job.

These things are worth thinking about both for your psyche and your pocketbook.

Proverbs 12:17 A good man is known by his truthfulness.... (The Living Bible)

One hour per day of study in your chosen field is all it takes. One hour per day of study will put you at the top of your field within three years. Within five years, you'll be a national authority. In seven years, you can be one of the best people in the world at what you do. Earl Nightingale

Answer a Question with a Question

W hen could you start the job?" I answered, "Next week." Then there was usually a pause and the person would say, "Oh! (pause) We won't be ready for about a month. I thought all the good contractors were booked up for several weeks. Are you not busy?"

This is where **Rule #24** came from.

Rule #24 – Answer a Question with a Question.

I learned to use this principle many years ago after being asked the above question. I hated that. It is so demeaning and condescending. I finally decided to ask this question in return, "When will you be ready?" That solved that problem. Sometimes they would totally forget the question they had asked and start talking about the job, their work or whatever and never asked me again. I could just say, "Well, call me a week or so ahead of time." Works like a champ every time. I taught my kids to do this, and then they tried it on me. I said, "Hey, I taught you that. Just answer straight up!"

Learn to ask questions or in other words get more information before answering. It helps save your sanity and makes you look like an expert. It feels much better, too.

These rules came from situations that I ran into over the last 40 years of contracting. They were the way I worked out to be as comfortable as possible in uncomfortable situations. They have kept me out of trouble and guarded me against loss many times.

Good habits keep you safe and defend you as you will see as we go through more of these rules.

Remember, these rules don't apply all the time. But if you make a habit of keeping them, you will see their wisdom.

Some particular jobs may require a slight alteration of some of these. But in talking to other contractors through the years, most have agreed they keep these same rules. There is a reason for different trades and professions coming to the same or similar conclusions.

Rules keep you, your business and your money safe. They help to establish your integrity, and they result in an internal confidence. You know what to do or say.

Rule #25 – Stand up for Yourself.

Stand up for yourself. Bold but not arrogant. No one else will stand up for you. In other words have a backbone. People will have more respect for you, and in the long run it will benefit your business because it gives off an air of confidence. Confident but not prideful. People would much rather hire or contract with a confident person than one that is unsure of him or herself.

Rule #26 – Never Sit in the Driveway.

I remember a few times I was done with a job, packed up and then relaxed in my truck for a few minutes before leaving -- filling out paperwork or making phone calls. Then at times I would hear a tap on my window and here was the client with a spot they found that they wanted me to look at. I would go with them back into the job I just left for maybe a couple of hours.

Most of the time the items were very small. So small in fact that if I was not there they would have never called me. Some people told me that if I had left they would not have bothered to call. I learned: don't sit in the driveway. Others I have talked to have learned that same thing. We are not trying to do shoddy work or get away with something, but some things are so insignificant it is almost laughable, but may take a couple of hours to fix if it is even possible. Make your calls from a gas station.

Rule #27 – Leave the Key in the Lock.

Many houses have a lockbox on the front door especially on construction sites. After you take the key from the lockbox and unlock the door, leave it in the door. Don't put it in your pocket. I have had to drive 30 minutes back to a job because I put the key in my pocket after I unlocked the door. I forgot and took the key with me. Usually, this happens because the house was locked when I got there, but before I was done, others showed up to work. You would not lock a door with people in the house, so if the key is in your pocket, you just forget and leave. Now you have to go back. Just leave the key in the door. This solves that problem. If no one is there when you leave, lock the house and put the key back. This makes life simpler.

We also follow these rules for locking houses:

- If the house is open when we get there between 8-5, we leave it open when we are finished.
- If the house is locked when we get there, we lock it when we leave.
- If the house is open when we get there but it is about 5:00 when we leave, we lock it up.

- Sometimes I will call the builder if I am unsure what he wants done.

Usually these lock rules work well. But you will get an occasional call of irritation. If they want it done differently, just say, "No problem," and do what they ask.

> As a side note: unless instructed to by the builder, NEVER give the house key to the buyer. Some people will move into the house before the closing date and then never close. I have been on several jobs where this occurred. In some cases, they lived there for months and had to be evicted. People can be very friendly and very deceitful. If the buyer insists you give them the keys, just tell them you are not authorized to give out keys to anyone and that they need to speak to the builder. If they tell you the builder said to give them the keys, call and verify.

Rule #28 – Establish Trust.

Establishing trust with your clients takes time. This is one reason it is important to dress appropriately for the first contact. I carry an ironed shirt on a hanger in the back seat, and on some jobs I put that on before I go to the door. First impressions are important.

You want to build a reputation for being honest and truthful. That kind of reputation will take you much further down the road and open up many doors that would otherwise be closed to you.

I had a foreman years ago that requested some work be done in his home. I asked how he wanted this to be billed, and he said to charge it to a house that was under construction. These situations are always a mess. I finally called his supervisor and asked him if this was company policy. He said, "NO!" I took the risk that the foreman might convince the building company to fire me in retaliation. I would rather be fired and lose that large account than gain a reputation of being dishonest. What would have happened if the main builder saw the bill, knew I had not worked on that house and when I told them about the foreman's request, the foreman denied everything? Then I would appear to be fleecing the builder. People talk!!

A reputation of dishonesty would be very hard to overcome if it ever could be. At times I have pointed out to people how I saved them money or that I was refunding money they gave me for parts. They would have never known that I did not use them. Sometimes I have to tell them I am just being honest by saying, "If it was mine, I would not spend the money on the repair. I would just replace the unit." Since I do not sell new units, I am just giving them my best advice.

Once you start down the road of lying, where do you stop? Once people know you lie, how can they ever trust you to tell the truth in the future? If you "fudge" a bill and send it to the manufacturer when the builder knows it really is his fault, where do you stop? You get a reputation for not being honest.

It may make you some friends in the short run, but in the long run it will destroy your business. People talk, and they will learn that they cannot trust what you say if they need an honest evaluation. You are a liar. Just be honest.

Rule #29 – Never Take Instructions from Anyone Other Than Who is Paying.

As I write this, I remember that about a week ago a general contractor reinstructed me on what he wanted me to repair. I looked him in the eye and politely said, "You are not the one paying me." He might be right in his instructions, but I will call and verify. I call and verify everything. I had two last week where the builder instructed me to do one repair, but the homeowner said there were three. I called and verified and was told to go ahead. But I have been told in the past, "No, we are only paying for one. The other is on them." So that is what you tell the homeowner. If the homeowner wants to argue, you just tell them they need to call and talk to the builder.

You need to call and verify on any instructions you receive from anyone that is not paying for the job.

I have had many builders thank me for verifying.

I looked at one person and said, "I don't even know who you are!!" Then I went and talked to the builder. That time it turns out that it was a real estate agent, and they had no idea what they were talking about. Always verify.

Rule #30 – Ask Who Is Paying for the Job, Part 1.

Most contractors are afraid to talk about money. You just have to get over it. Before you even start the job, settle the question of payment. Who is paying for the job? I ask this over the phone many times. If they say another person is paying, I ask for that person's phone number and verify. We try to verify everything. I have run into many situations where all the parties involved said they were not paying. I told each person they needed to talk to each other and have the one that is paying call me back.

If you settle this up front, you will have fewer problems. But if you wait till afterwards, they may all say, "Thanks," but leave you holding an empty sack. We will talk more about money in some of the later rules.

Rule #31 – Always Return Your Phone Calls or Reply to Text Messages Promptly.

I will never forget the first client I picked up as a contractor. I asked her what happened to her other contractor. She said, "I can never get him to call me back or answer the phone." Many times I have been told the person called me because they could not get a hold of their regular contractor -- sometimes for a couple of months. You can pick up a lot of business over time by just returning calls. People like doing business with those they can get in contact with quickly. Also, this is good marketing. On my business card for years I had the phrase: "We return calls promptly."

Proverbs 25:13 Like the cold of snow in the time of harvest is a faithful messenger to those who send him; he refreshes the soul of his masters.
(English Standard Version)

"Winning is a habit. Watch your thoughts, they become your beliefs. Watch your beliefs, they become your words. Watch your words, they become your actions. Watch your actions, they become your habits. Watch your habits, they become your character." Vince Lombardi

CHAPTER 14

We Don't Pick Up Checks!

Many years ago, I was waiting in the outer office of a builder with about 20 other contractors. It was Friday afternoon about 2:20. A door opens, and the lady says, "We are not giving you your checks until after 3:00, so stop asking."

I had picked up checks several times on Friday afternoon. This day I asked myself, "What are you doing here with these people?" I did not like the picture it painted of my business nor did I like being treated that way. I did not like the feelings I had in me being there. It was demeaning. I never picked up another check on Fridays again.

When you wait in line as a contractor to pick up checks on Fridays, it gives off the impression that you cannot make it through the weekend without the money. It says you cannot manage your money well enough to run your business without getting a check on Friday.

Learn to leave enough in your accounts to make it until the middle of the next week when the checks come in. You can do it. It is just what you allow in your life and what you get used to.

So from then on we asked to have the checks mailed and never picked them up again. This is where **Rule #32** came from.

Rule #32 – We Don't Pick up Checks!

This freed me up to do more jobs on Friday afternoon and increased our bottom line.

Rule #33 – Take Care of Call Backs Immediately.

No one is perfect. If you messed up a job and get a call back to correct it, take care of it immediately especially if it's for a major account. Fix it within the first 24 hours or sooner so they know that you can be counted on to take care of problems when they come up. This is great for your reputation.

Repairing the goof ASAP also makes your mistake leave their mind quickly. You don't need the thought of your screw up lingering in their head.

Don't argue over $25 or $100 especially when you make $1,500 - $5,000/year from that account. Don't argue over pennies; you lose dollars, so just fix it. It will save you a ton of headaches when you go looking for new accounts.

I have read that UPS has representatives that have the OK to write a check for $100.00 to any client that is upset his box did not arrive on time. This is with large corporate accounts that may ship many boxes each week. One box may cost only $15.00 to ship so why a $100.00 refund? That business may spend several thousand dollars a year shipping so why lose a good account over such a small amount.

So we adopted the phrase, "No problem!" If someone does call with a complaint, I just say, "No problem. I will take care of it tomorrow or sometime that day." No arguing, nor hard feelings, EVER! Their business is worth much more than one silly job even if it is not your fault. Do you want to be right or make money? Just do it over and make it right with a smile on your face. Have some plastic surgery done if you have to, but smile!!!

Rule #34 – Eat That Frog.

I listen to Brian Tracy some, and he has a set of CD's called <u>Eat That Frog</u>. The idea is to do the worst job or the job you dread doing the most first thing in the morning or the week.

To paraphrase Mr. Tracy – think of it as a frog you have to eat live today. If you eat it first thing in the morning, then it is over with. That is far better than dreading the thought of eating it all day long and then finally eating it at 5:00 PM. Do it first thing in the morning, and it is over with. The rest of the day is free. Very nice!

Sometimes I do the call backs first. I hate those. Or I call the jobs with cranky people first.   There can be any number of reasons you dread doing certain jobs, but no matter, do them first thing, and it greatly reduces your stress for the day.

If that idea works for you, buy the set of CD's from Brian Tracy as a way of saying thank you. They are interesting and fun to listen to as you drive around.

Rule #35 – Don't Stay on Hold for Too Long.

Staying on hold too long is like you are begging, like you have nothing better to do while they take care of THEIR business.

- If they called you, let them call back.
- If you called them, wait a couple of hours then call back.

Apologize, and say you could not wait but had to go -- pressing issues.

Like it or not life is a lot about impressions. If you stay on hold long, it gives the impression that you are not busy. I would rather leave the impression I am very busy, thus, **very good at what I do**, even if I have nothing else to do. **Think about it!**

Rule #36 – Do an Extra Job Each Day.

Do an extra job each day if your jobs are short. You will be shocked at the end of the month how much better your accounts look. Something I learned from a wise old man was to tell God how much you want to make each day. Tape it to your rearview mirror. Just a number. Keep it to yourself, and each day ask Him to help you reach that goal.

If you put jobs off until tomorrow, the time will come when you will be buried in jobs because you are behind and a diligent competitor will pick up your work. Don't become complacent!

Rule #37 – Use the 80/20 Rule.

When I was young, I did this with my grass mowing accounts. At the beginning of each year, I culled the ones that only wanted the grass cut every other week so that it was tall and very time consuming to do with no extra money. I would also cull the ones that did not want to pay more because their yard was too large for the price they were paying.

You can use this rule for any wholesalers, other contractors or manufacturers that you work for. Most people are great, but some just need to go.

This 80/20 rule is old, and the principle is found in many different areas of life. The following link can help you to understand some of how it works:

https://en.wikipedia.org/wiki/Pareto_principle

- 20% of your customers will give you 80% of your grief. When the time is right, cull them.

- 20% of your customers will give you 80% of your income. They go to the top of the list for priority when you make out your schedule.

Rules guard our lives – our minds. They help guard, most importantly, our minds from feeling frustrated, defeated, used or belittled. This is important because the more you have these feelings, you are likely to see yourself as not worth much.

Rules also help guard our integrity in the minds of others. They will begin to realize that you run a business and are not just someone that needs to buy groceries for their family.

Many people have a very poor attitude toward contractors. Looking at some of the contractors out there, that is understandable. So it takes a little work on your part to set yourself apart from the other contractors in general and to set yourself apart from those in your field. Self-imposed rules of conduct can help you accomplish that very quickly.

Self-imposed rules of conduct help your self-image, help your self-confidence, and they give you a predetermined path to follow in situations that could cause you to feel inadequate or intimidated. A good way to deflect some of what people say to you is to tell them that this it is company policy. If I don't follow that policy, my boss will fire me. Then if I need more help in deflecting, I will tell them, "Yes, my wife is my boss, and I'd like to stay married."

Proverbs 10:4 He becometh poor that dealeth with a slack hand;
but the hand of the diligent maketh rich. (KJV)

CHAPTER 15

Go Get the Money, Part 1

Rule #38 – Go Get the Money!

I was talking to a plumber a week ago, and he told me about a job he did six months back in a wealthy neighborhood for about $650. They still had never sent him a check. I told him I would be calling them four to five times a day. But he apparently just let it go.

On the other hand, I spoke to a fire chief in a town southwest of here about three years ago. He told me the ambulance service in their town was about $2.8 million in the red a few years back. The city had no idea why, so they put the ambulance service under the authority of the fire department.

When the fire department looked at the books and the method for collecting past due accounts, they found the problem. The lady in charge of collecting for the ambulance service called the people one time if they had not paid, and then put the bill in the non-collectible file. She never called them again.

Well, the fire department changed that. He did not say they sued anyone, but they sent them letters and made phone calls until the bills were paid. They went and GOT THE MONEY! The ambulance service was back in the black in about 1½ years. **Diligence makes a huge difference.** It can be the difference between prosperity and going out of business.

Collecting money is one of the most uncomfortable things about being a contractor. Sometimes collecting your money involves confrontation, and confrontation is something that most people avoid like the plague.

If you don't GO GET THE MONEY, it is not fair to you. You did the work. AND it is not fair to your family. You are working and spending time away from the ones you love and care for – and not getting paid. NO! If that has been you in the past on some accounts, you need to change that immediately. So you have to do some thinking about how to so set up your relationship with your customers so that you get paid 999 times out of a 1,000.

In the last 40 years, I have been cheated out of about $2000. That is a very small amount compared to what I have had others tell me they have lost. That amount is so low because we GO GET THE MONEY! Many contractors will tell you stories of losing $1,000's on a single job.

There are many things you can do to put the odds in your favor. Some we have already discussed in previous rules. We will have some more rules still to come.

Rule #39 – No Waiting on Third Parties to Pay Your Customer.

I always ask, "Who is paying?" on certain jobs. Sometimes I hear:

- "Do the work now, then send us a bill, and you will get paid at the closing of the house." Some deals fall through, then who pays? Or they put off the closing for three more weeks. Or the seller does not get what they expected at closing and can't pay.

What if the seller "forgets"?

- "Do the work and when the insurance company pays us, we will pay you." What if the insurance company does not pay for that? How long will that be? Way too many variables.

- "Do the work, and the manufacturer will pay or the store will pay or the carpenter will pay."

Or they say, "Send the bill to the builder or the plumber."

The reason they don't want to pay but want to wait for someone else to come up with the money is because they feel they should not have to pay for the work no matter what. And if someone is going to get stuck with no money, they would rather have it be you and not them. If the other entity does not pay, neither will they. Just so you know.

NO! We tell them we need to be paid when the work is done. We can email them a receipt and an invoice, and **they** can collect from the third party. Our company policy does not allow us to wait on ....

I have a friend in the same business as I am in a small town east of here. He did about $3,000 worth of work in some apartments. When he was finished, the owner, a local, would not pay. No reason, he just would not pay. So then my friend (the contractor) filed a lien on the property. About three years later, an attorney called him and said that the building was being sold, and they needed to clear up the lien the contractor had on the building. The attorney said he had a check for $1500 at his office the contractor could pick up for signing a lien release.

You see, many people think contractors are poor business men and just barely able to keep food on the table, so they would jump at the chance to at least get $1500.00 out of a three year old bill. The contractor told the attorney he could make out the check for the $3,000 plus the filing fees and the interest or he would not sign anything. The attorney said, "That's not happening." Two weeks later, the attorney called back with a check for the right amount. Backbone and patience pay well.

If you are going to have a business, you need to run it like a business!

Rule #40 – Collect Money up Front for Parts.

On any job where you need to order parts, we collect the retail price of the parts up front. Why? After you have ordered the parts or received them, the customer may cancel the work request. Why?

- People may decide to move instead of repairing the unit.
- They may decide to replace unit.
- Their neighbor fixed it for free, etc.
- Their mother died, and they are putting the project on hold indefinitely.
- People have a myriad of excuses.

Now you have parts you can't use, and many companies charge a 20% restocking fee plus postage. Why should you be out that money? If they have any objection to paying for the parts up front because they do not know if they can trust you, tell them they need to find someone they can trust because **your business requires that the parts be paid for in advance**. Usually people don't have a problem with collecting for parts before ordering and will send you a check in the mail if you talk over the phone.

I have told people, "I have lived in the same house for 30 years and had the same phone number for that long, too. I work for many well-known businesses and that if I were unreliable, I would be out of business very quickly. But I can understand their apprehension. "Talk to your spouse and if you still want the parts, then let me know." Leave the ball on their side of the court. Most of the time they will call you back. There is no pressure in handling it that way. They can send the check in the mail or call you with a credit card number.

When it comes to pricing parts, we usually have them pay retail for the parts up front and let them know we will add any tax and shipping to the final invoice when we come to do the repair. Some of the manufacturers I work for have their pricing schedule set up that way.

We pay the manufacturer $50.00, and the retail price is $100.00. This is very fair. Why?

- We have to receive it in the mail.
- We have to enter the amount into the books on the computer.
- We have to deposit it in the bank.
- If the customer cancels the work order, we now have the funds to return it to the manufacturer and still not be out any money. If the manufacturer requires a 20% restocking fee, our restocking fee is 30% plus postage both ways to cover our office expenses in handling the transaction we did in both receiving the parts and shipping them back.
- Finally, it gives a profit on our business. Without a profit, you go out of business!

As a side note, most good interior designers require 50% of the cost of the goods before ordering and the other 50% **on delivery.** Usually, the 50% on ordering covers the cost of the goods. This is very common.

Don't do things for free. This is a business!

Remember you are running a business not a charity!

Rule #41 – Call about the Bill the Next Day.

When you send a bill to a <u>first-time</u> client, whether it is faxed or emailed, call them the next day and ask them if they received it. If yes, ask them when they will pay if you do not already know. If you know how they pay, confirm that over the phone. "Since it is in before Wednesday, you will cut us a check on Friday. Is that right?" If you do not receive a check by the following Tuesday, call them again, and ask them if they mailed it. <u>The longer you let an invoice go without contacting the customer, the longer they will take to pay</u>. It may be that they realize that you avoid confrontation, so they pay others first and let yours slide.

This process establishes your presence as one who expects to be paid and expects them to do what they have said.

Proverbs 10:4 He becometh poor that dealeth with a slack hand: but the hand of the diligent maketh rich.(KJV)

Our deepest fear is not that we are inadequate. Our deepest fear is that we are powerful beyond measure. It is our light, not our darkness that most frightens us. We ask ourselves, "Who am I to be brilliant, gorgeous, talented, fabulous?" Actually, who are you not to be? You are a child of God. Your playing small does not serve the world. There is nothing enlightened about shrinking so that other people won't feel insecure around you. We are all meant to shine, as children do. We are born to make manifest the glory of God that is within us. It is not just in some of us; it is in everyone. And as we let our own light shine, we unconsciously give other people permission to do the same. As we are liberated from our own fear, our presence automatically liberates others. Marianne Williamson

Go Get the Money, Part 2!

Many years ago I was involved in a large job with an interior designer. She told me up front that she would be paying for the labor of what I was doing. It was quite a large job, and I was there for a while. In talking to the other contractors, I found that this designer was footing the bill for the entire remodel herself with no upfront money from the homeowner. She paid for the remodeling, the carpet, the wallpaper, and all other materials. All the labor for the trades was going to be paid by her once the job was completed and she got paid.

In talking to the homeowner, I learned that he was a workman's comp attorney. From what I know of this type of attorney, all they do is sue people, and they are the most likely of all attorneys to not pay once the job is complete.

This job was making me nervous, so when I was done, I talked the decorator into letting me bill the homeowner myself. She finally agreed. Then I spoke with the attorney. He said all bills were to go through the decorator. I told him that yes, that was true but that she had told me I could bill him directly myself. He finally agreed, and I went that night and picked up a check from him. When the job was finally done, the decorator and the attorney had a falling out over the bill, and I don't know if she ever got paid.

She should have required the homeowner to pay one-half of the price of the materials upfront before ordering. With her markup that should have covered 100% of her cost. Then the other half should have been paid on delivery - on delivery not installation. As she was making no money off the labor, she should have had the homeowner pay for the labor from each contractor on completion of their work.

Dividing large jobs into small bite size chunks for payment will prevent many problems with collections.

That is where **Rule #42** came from.

Rule #42 – Don't Work for Lawyers.

Some lawyers only pay by lawsuits. This week I spoke to a painter that had been burned by a lawyer recently. When you find out it's a lawyer, bid the job too high or tell them you just don't have the time at the moment to do the work and let that job slide -- even if you are not busy. Busy without getting paid is a sickening feeling. Better to go fishing and pray than to deal with the stress of being stiffed.

Rule #43 – Ask Who is Paying for the Job, Part 2.

We ask up front, "Are you paying for this or is someone else?" By asking this question, I have heard, "I am not paying; this is a new house. The builder, plumber or manufacturer is paying." Ask for the phone number of the person they said was paying **and verify**. I have had several times where the builder said, "I gave them your number to do the work, but I am not paying."

I forgot to ask on one job a few years ago. In order to have access to the malfunctioning parts, we had the builder take the brick off the outside of the house and then take the sheeting and insulation out. In the process of repairing the unit, I found out from the wife that the unit had no warranty. I stopped working and called the builder to see if he was paying. "NO!" He said the plumber was. I called the plumber and he said, "NO! I thought I bought a good unit and that the wholesaler was paying." Well, the wholesaler said that the manufacturer's warranty was up two years earlier, and there was no way they were going to pay.

So I leaned a piece of plywood over the hole, called the builder and told him they needed to figure out who was paying since there was no warranty and call me back. Two weeks later the plumber called and said he was paying because the builder threatened to fire him if the plumber did not pay to fix the unit. (Personally, if I had been the plumber, I would have told the builder to stuff it, but a lot of people don't stand up for themselves.)

If I had finished the work then found that out that no one was paying, it would have been very hard to collect. Don't get caught in that trap. Always discuss the money issue up front. Most people have no problem with discussing payments up front. The people that do have a problem with it are the ones you want to watch.

I have also found that if you are willing and open to discuss the payment issue up front, they have more respect for you and getting paid becomes a far smaller problem than it might have been. They see and respect your confidence and may decide to ply their non-payment craft on someone else.

It is always uncomfortable, but the feelings of not getting paid are far worse.

Rule #44 – Tell People Up Front What the Cost is Going to Be.

This way there are no surprises for them. And they can't come back with mock surprise at the cost to make you feel bad and reduce the price after the job is finished. It may be uncomfortable talking about money before the job is started, but if you want to eliminate collection problems, you have to do it.

Rule #45 – We Get Paid on Completion of a Commercial Job.

Many years ago I was working late one night in a mall and talking to the carpet layer and the subject of getting paid came up. He said he was getting a check that night when he was done. "How did you do that?" I asked. He had told them that was the only way he would do the job. WOW! I never forgot that.

It took us four months to get paid by that Wisconsin company.

As we started to do more commercial jobs in the business we are in now, I incorporated the same idea.

I tell them up front we can do the job, but we need to be paid the day we are done. Can they write me a check? Many times writing a check is difficult for them to do, so I tell them a credit card will work. I tell them to talk to their boss and let me know. Many commercial jobs have company credit cards on site. I have never been turned down.

The problem with billing on commercial jobs is that most of the time their offices are out of state. I have been told, "Well, I send the invoice to Arkansas and the job super signs off on it, then it goes to accounting in Alabama, then the Partner in New York has to review it and write the check but the checks are sent from California, and there is no way for me to tell you what part of the process your invoice is in."

Meanwhile, the contractor has finished the job and left the state. The foreman I talked to has changed jobs and works for someone else.

Sometimes you are left with no one to contact and no phone numbers. We have had to look the company up on the internet to find out how to contact their accounting department.

I would rather lose the job than go through that to collect the money.

We do the same on any out of town job. They pay while we are there or we don't go. We settle that issue up front. I tell them all, "It is nothing personal; it is just the best way we have found to not have to spend our time chasing money." Most understand and will arrange it for you.

Also, I have had local entities where the bills are paid from some out of state company. We ask them to have a check sent to the local company, and then they give it to us on completion of the job. You just have to have the attitude that I do not want to chase that money down.

This works for small companies with small bills. If you are a larger contractor, you have to find ways to take care of the problem. Every business will have a way to collect in a timely manner.

Once you adopt the attitude that you **will** get paid, you will find that you get paid much more often. Even if the amount is small, it is the principle of the thing. You deserve to be paid, so don't give up. Be a thorn in their side until they take care of the bill.

One contractor I talked to sends them a final letter stating that they will be turned over to a collection agency in seven days if the bill is not paid. He states that the collection agency's fee will be attached to the bill, and they may notify the credit bureaus.

Another method I have seen involves a set of letters on this web site: http://stevensricci.com/collection-letters/.

However you deal with collecting, remember, you deserve to be paid. Ignore the negative things that people will say and just stick to your course. You will become less uncomfortable with talking about the money up front over time. **Remember, your family deserves your best effort.**

Whatever you do will become a habit. If you develop the habit of allowing people to not pay, you will lose thousands of dollars that you worked for over your life time.

The first thing I ALWAYS do if my wife gives me an account to collect is pray and ask God to help me resolve the issue. I firmly believe that God has saved my A** many times over the years where otherwise I would have gone away with an empty sack. Ask me about them sometime, and I will tell you those stories, too.

Not hateful or arrogant just purposeful and bold. A mind set like a rock.

The longer you are willing to wait to get paid, the longer they will take to pay!

Learning to stick up for yourself and being bold is all part of The Prosperous Life.

Proverbs 28:1 .... But the righteous are bold as a lion (KJV)

CHAPTER 17

The Accountant Has My Checkbook!

Some people just won't pay until you call them. Some won't pay until you call, email or fax several times. So in our business, my wife does the collecting. (Home owners pay the day the work is done.) If they have not paid in the time reasonable for their classification, she calls them on the phone and simply asks if they received the invoice. It is usually two weeks for builders, two weeks for plumbers, two months for manufacturers, and two months for wholesalers. Then be quiet and see what they say. Sometimes it is amazing the excuses they give.

- My secretary had it in her purse and forgot to mail it for two weeks.
- The accountant has my checkbook.
- We changed our fax number.
- We changed our email address.
- We never got that invoice.
- We decided not to pay.
- We sent it to the plumber.
- The homeowner is supposed to pay, and we have not gotten the money yet.
- I thought we already paid that.
- And the best one: Plumber, "Well, my guy did that mistake so I am not paying." I said, "Well, he works for you!" Response, "Not anymore; he stole my pickup and ran off with my daughter, so I fired him. If you want your money, talk to him." (We got the money, but it took many calls to the plumber and the builder.

Sometimes it is like dealing with small children. This was also an out of town job, and from then on out of town builders, plumbers and clients have to pay on the spot or we won't do the work. It is more difficult to collect on out of town jobs than local jobs. Just tell the out of town client that it is nothing personal, but on out of town jobs our company policy is we need to be paid while we are there or we cannot do the work. I sleep much better that way. **If there is one thing I hate in life, it is not getting paid.**)

When my wife emails or faxes an invoice, she writes or types across the face of the invoice the date it was emailed or faxed. So by the fifth time, there are several dates. (Faxed 2/03/2107; emailed 2/15/17; emailed......)

If she is not successful in collecting the money, she gives it to me. I am not usually as polite as my wife. I am successful most all of the time. I have called some people over 100 times.

In the past, I know they do not answer if they see it is my number, so I will borrow other people's phones and call. I reach them eventually.

I called the last one three times before 10:00 AM.

- The first time I called (7:15 AM), I told him we needed to get these invoices taken care of as they were two months old.
- The second call, I left no message since he will see it is my number.
- The third call, I simply asked him to call me.

He called 30 minutes later. He apologized and asked how he could take care of it. I said he could use a credit card, as I have an app on my phone. In two minutes the bill was paid. It is amazing how easily people will pay with a credit card.

You just have to accept the fact that confrontation is the name of the game if you want to get paid and your family deserves to have the money you worked for. We are not a charity nor are we donating our labor so others can have their projects done at a lower cost.

We have had this rule of Keep Calling until You Get the Money for 40 years. It has worked out very well. It takes some guts, and it is uncomfortable, but the feeling of not being paid is sickening. Thus, **Rule #46.**

Rule #46 – Keep Calling!

In residential jobs where there is a homeowner, a simple way to avoid collections is to settle, up front, how you will be paid. Ask them if they will be paying with a check or credit card. If they will not be there when the work is done, ask them if they can leave you a check as your company does not bill residential customers. For instance, has the plumber ever offered to send you a bill in the mail? No! You pay him on the spot. You should expect the same.

Get a credit card app for your phone and offer to have them pay by credit card. It will cost you 2-3.5 %, but that is a small price to pay for not having to call to collect later. We use the Intuit app Go Payment. You may have to also use QuickBooks to get that app. Square works also, but they are progressives and many politically incorrect things they do not allow to go through their app.

We have done some jobs where we are paid with a credit card when we are done by calling them on the phone.

Rule #47 – Don't Allow People to Make You Feel Guilty for Collecting.

People are great manipulators. Some will try to make you feel guilty for asking about your money. **Never feel guilty!** Those people are the ones you may want to put on the 20% list that cause you 80% of your grief. Lose them!

I stopped by a builder's home many years ago on a Saturday morning and asked for a check. This was during a very depressed time in the housing market. She said, "Can you never wait?" I said, "Hey, I was in the area." (I was in the area TO COLLECT A CHECK!) She paid, and I learned later that on the following Tuesday the bank turned her down for her last draw. I was the last person to get paid 100% of their bill. We made it by one day or less. The rest of the contractors took 20 cents on the dollar two years later. I believe God fights for me and gives me the boldness that is required to get paid at times.

The righteous are bold as a lion. Bold but not rude. Bold but not pushy or arrogant.

You did the work and deserve to be paid. If the agreement is to be paid the day you are done, expect that to happen.

I have been on jobs where the homeowner was there every day all day long until Friday when it was apparent you would be finishing up. Then about 2:00, they are just gone. Now you are finished, and they are not to be found anywhere.

Check with them on the day the job is going to be completed. Ask, "Are you going to be here when I'm done so you can write me a check?" If they mumble, rephrase what they just said. "Are you saying that you'll be here this afternoon to give me a check when I'm done?"

The practice of rephrasing works for a good many things to set in stone what was agreed upon.

If they won't be there, explain you need to be paid before you leave, so could they write it just before they go. Once people give their word, many times it changes the situation, and they do the right thing.

In many situations, asking whether they want to pay with a check or a credit card is much better than just asking for a check. "Do you want to pay with a check or a credit card before you leave?" Done properly they will answer with one or the other. It is a sales technique that works well to close a conversation.

Collecting money is one of the most uncomfortable things about being a contractor. Sometimes collecting your money involves confrontation, and confrontation is something that most people avoid like the plague.

If you don't GO GET THE MONEY, it is not fair to you. You did the work. AND it is not fair to your family. You are working and spending time away from the ones you love and care for — and not getting paid? NO. If that has been you in the past on some accounts, you need to change that immediately. So you have to do some thinking about how to so set up your relationship with your customers so that you get paid 99.99% of the time.

Learning how to get paid on every job is an art, and it is all part of The Prosperous Life.

Proverbs 14:24 The wise accumulate wisdom; fools get stupider by the day.
(The Message)

Invest three percent of your income in yourself (self-development) in order to guarantee your future. Brian Tracy

CHAPTER 18

Never Accept a Beer from a Client

Then he said, "I thought all contractors were drunks."

I was working late one night in a home when the homeowner offered me a beer. He was very friendly and we had been chatting quite a bit while I was working. But I declined. Then he offered me some whiskey which I thought was odd and declined it also. Then he said, "I thought all contractors were drunks!" He was not what he seemed to be. Many people are like that.

To drink on a job is not smart at all no matter how tired you are, how hot it is, or if other people are drinking beer. Some companies will fire you on the spot if they catch you. This is where **Rule #48** comes from.

Rule #48 – Never Accept a Beer from a Client.

It does your reputation no good if you are found to accept a drink while working. You may think no one else will ever know. Brian Tracy taught the truth that everyone knows everything. People will eventually know you do that and so will all your suppliers and professional contacts. It could spell disaster for your business in the long run.

Rule #49 – We Only Will Wait 10 to 15 Minutes.

I called a client on one job, and he said he could meet me. I got there and waited about five minutes and then called him to "see how far out he was." Really, I called to see if he had left work yet because sometimes they haven't.

He said he got tied up but would be there in about 10 minutes. At 12 minutes, I called again. (I usually write the time down on a clip board that I carry, so I remember what time he said that.) Then he tells me he is leaving in a few minutes. What he is really doing is trying to get me to wait till he gets off work. He said, "Can't you wait for a bit?" I said, "No. I have other jobs to do."

It was a couple of weeks before I called him back. The next time he was prompt.

He never intended to meet me. He wanted to string me along until he got off work. We don't wait.

Sometimes people will want to meet at 4:00 PM. You can ask, "Do you want to meet at 4:00 or is that when you get off work?" If they won't actually be there until 4:30, we decline and wait for another day.

If you wait much longer than 15 minutes, it appears as though you have nothing else to do other than wait on them to be able to make some money. It gives a very poor image of you and your business.

Rule #50 – Only Reschedule Once.

If you have to reschedule a job, only do it once. More than one reschedule makes you look flakey besides the fact that many people look down on contractors as being unreliable. It also gives the appearance that you can't run a good schedule or a good business.

The reputation you want to build is that if you say it, you will do it and on time. People will pay more for that than great workmanship.

Rule #51 – Be on Time.

Some people are always late, and they will tell you so. If you are late, hey, that is how they are, and it is very acceptable.

But there is a class of people out there that prize punctuality. If you are late, they will never call you again. That is just how they see life. You are unreliable, and you will not put forth the effort to be on time.

So if you want all the work you can get, be on time and get those "clock watchers," too!

Having said that, the only other acceptable thing that works is to call or text them and tell them you will be late. It is not quite as good, but it is much better that just showing up late. Some people won't wait long if you are not on time. So if it happens – call.

Rule #52 – Never Go into Homes with Only Young Children, Especially Girls.

This rule came up again this week. The lady told me that if I beat her to the house, her daughter would let me in. I told her I would wait.

It is just good policy. Another time, I was working out of town on a job. I had called the man and verified the time I would be there. I got to the house and an 8-10 year old girl answered the door. She said her dad had called and said to let us in (I had a helper with me), and that her dad would be there shortly.

I told her we would wait in the truck. I told the man who was the local fire chief that we never enter a house with only underage girls there. He said he understood.

Sometimes you have to find out if the young person is a boy or girl and what age they are. Boys are not quite the problem. You could ask if they go to college. If not, tell them, "It's nothing personal; it is just against our company policy to go into homes with only young girls there unless they have graduated from high school. I need the adult to meet us. Most people will understand.

What I don't understand is instructing a young girl to let an adult into their home that they have never met. It seems odd to me, but people do it.

Rule #53 – Go Get the Work.

If you want the work, you have to go get it. Figure out every possible avenue that could use what you do. Then call or go by and drop off some cards.

- Manufacturers
- Wholesalers
- Tradesmen
- Apartment complexes
- Real estate agents
- Builders

I found a list of all the builders in our area online in the beginning which was about 400 people. I entered them all into a data base, so that we could print out envelopes and have them look nice. Then we mailed them all letters.

This was a lot of work, but every time I did that we would pick up two or three builders. If you do that four times a year, it will pay off after a while.

Spend some time on the phone calling people that could benefit from your business especially if they are out of town. I picked up some accounts on the fourth call.

Always look for a way to pick up more business. I did a job for a wholesaler years ago. When I was done, I called him on the phone and visited with him. I asked him what brands he sold. He mentioned one that I did not work for and I told him that. He said that they had just hired a new salesman and gave me the man's number. A few weeks later I was in with that brand and have done a number of jobs over the years and also gotten a great many referrals.

Finally, pray and ask God to open doors for you. He will because He is your Father. If God is not your Father, then get born again and then pray. He will be able to be more help to you than you can ever imagine.

> Side note on marketing: Find out what your competitors are poor at, and use that to market your business.

> For instance: I found when I first started that many will not return phone calls promptly. So I marketed that we did. Some people just want a return call. Ask them.

> When you pick up a new client, after a bit ask them why they stopped using the other service. Use that in your marketing. When I asked one builder why he switched, he said "We wanted our warranty work taken care of quickly, and you do that." It was that simple. Good habits pay in spades.

Rule #54 – Keep Your Foot in Both Sides of the Market.

You never know when the market will reverse, and you will need that other part of the market. I have worked in new construction for years, but there have been times when housing starts were nonexistent. Then the remodel market is important. When one part is up, the other part is down. Keep a foot in both. Nothing lasts forever.

> Side note: Any downturn in the market will be a good time to pick up new business. Many will go out of business because they do not follow good marketing principles, and you can clean up. If they go out of business, buy their phone numbers from the phone company and expand yourself.

Rule #55 – Practice Self-Development.

Buy at least one personal development course per year. Listen and learn. (Jim Rohn - All of his cd's)

Buy books on marketing.

Buy books on how to sell because most of your business is selling yourself and your business. (Brian Tracy)

Buy a Bible and read the book of Proverbs over and over.

Rule #56 – Tell Them What to Expect.

I have found that you prevent a lot of trouble during and after a job by telling people what to expect during the job -- noise, dust, delays, etc. I also tell them what to expect the job to look like when it is completed. Explain everything up front even the objectionable things.

Then when those things come up, they will feel more like you were being honest with them. If they have to ask about those things when they see them and don't like them, then any explanation you give will seem like you are schmoozing (bullsh…ing) them or feeding them a line to get away with poor workmanship.

Think about it!

Rule #57 – We Don't Give Discounts.

Today, I found this rule that I had written under a file called Rules for Contractors! I had written it many years ago. A friend of mine and I were having an online discussion with another female contractor that was being asked to discount her work. We were both in agreement that we never discount our work. The reasoning here is the same as some of the other rules. If you discount your work, you fall into the category of contractors that "need" the work. I have had new builders that said, "I am building my own home first, then I will have several more for you to work in, so I need a builder's discount." I told them we price our work the same to everyone. Then you can add whatever statement you want after that. For example:

- It takes us just as long to do one job as another, and our overhead is the same no matter what the price.
- Our pricing is to the bone already, and we just can't.
- My boss would fire me if I gave you a discount without consulting her first. Yes, my wife is my boss, and she is mean. I would like to stay married, so I just can't.
- Whatever it takes. If possible, price their work higher. You probably don't want to work for them anyway.

That person that you give the discount to will most likely be one of your hardest clients to work for. But if you stick to your guns, that same client will most likely leave you to your work if they hire you.

Think about it!

Lastly, to end this set of rules, I wanted to take a minute and talk about money. Again! When I looked at the number of rules that dealt with money, the thought I had was that maybe I had money on the brain. We have covered things like: how to set up your payments, how to collect, the attitude you need, you need to be determined to get paid and you need to have a confident backbone....

But consider what God has to say about dealing with people in His Word.

> Jeremiah 22:13 Woe unto him that buildeth his house by unrighteousness, and his chambers by wrong; *that* useth his neighbour's service without wages, and giveth him not for his work;

Apparently, contractors not getting paid has been a problem for thousands of years. It is not a new thing. God says, "Woe to him that does not pay."

Why do people not want to pay? Not good quality work. They should have investigated the contractor before they hired them. Notice that in the verse that God makes no exceptions for not paying. Some people always find something wrong with the job so that they feel justified in not paying the full amount. So this is why many of the rules work together to give you a greater percentage of jobs that pay with no question. Then we have rules for the ones that are left that are difficult. Many people just don't like parting with their money.

Remember, some of the things we have covered in these rules. They all work together to increase your percentage of paying jobs. Because the nature of some people is to let you work for free!

- Dress well.
- Be on time.
- Explain the pricing up front and don't budge from it.
- Get used to confrontation.
- Settle the question of payment up front.
- Never back up on a bid.

Think about it!

Rule #58 – Pray.

Praying and asking God for help in expanding your work, collecting your bills and all other aspects of your business will give you a much more blessed life. I hope you have seen the wisdom of prayer throughout this book.

Psalm 34:15 The eyes of the LORD are upon the righteous, and his ears are open unto their cry.

Some Notes on Dealing with People

This one does not have a rule as such, but it is interesting.

Three or four times when I was younger, I had people call me and say "It's 10:00, we had an appointment for 9:00, and I took off work to meet you. Are you coming?"

At first I told them I was sorry and rushed over and did the work. I could not remember making the appointment, but since I talk to a lot of people maybe I did.

After this occurred three or four times over a couple of years, I began to realize I never set that appointment. So I began to ask them who they talked with to set this appointment. They usually responded with "your office, the job foreman or the manufacturer." I tell them that I am the only one to talk to get service. I will call you in the next few days, and we will figure out a time.

What probably happened is that they took off from work that morning for whatever reason, and it was convenient for them to have me come that morning. Rather than asking, they tried to guilt me into doing the job right now. That worked a few times but no longer.

Working in People's Homes

If you work in homes, here is something to consider: Many people, especially women, find it disturbing to have strangers working in their home, some to a greater degree and some lesser. Or even if you know them, it is difficult to have their home torn up for remodeling or even to have a garbage disposal installed. It is their home. It disrupts their routine. You have invaded their safe space so to speak. Most detest the mess even if you clean up somewhat. It is just disconcerting to them even if they say nothing. They can be uncomfortable. What helps is to be dressed well, use tarps, be polite and be on time. Get the job done and leave.

One of the very successful companies here in the City a few years ago advertised that their guys were well dressed and polite even though they were PLUMBERS. Dirty plumbers with grease on them and muddy boots are almost a proverb. It is accepted as the norm many times.

Well, this company charge $25 - $30 extra per hour because of the way they presented their employees at the door and on the job, and people were happy to pay.

Think about it!

Final Thoughts
Where in the River Did You Choose to Stand?

Several years ago I was doing a small job in a home not far from here. The man was telling me he was recently retired from a local prison where he had been employed as a shop teacher of sorts. He taught plumbing, electrical and trim carpentry.

Now that he was retired, he was going to work as a trim carpenter. Apparently, he was not licensed for electrical or plumbing. He told me he did not think it was fair that plumbers and electricians charged about $100 - $125.00 per hour, but as a trim carpenter all he could get was about $25.00 per hour.

I did not say anything, but it reminded me of what I had been taught a few years earlier by a wise man. He said the economy of money is like a river flowing through life. In the center of the river, the water is deep and like a raging torrent, but on the edges it is shallow and very slow moving. Each of us comes to the river with our bucket expecting to fill it with money.

No one tells us where to stand in the river to fill our buckets. Some stand in the middle where the buckets fill quickly, and some struggle to fill their buckets in the shallow edges.

The man could have put in the time to become licensed as a plumber or an electrician, but he chose to be a trim carpenter.

If you don't like the part of the river you are in, CHANGE PLACES. Go study what the successful people do, and stand where they do.

Think about it!

Always remember, ask God for knowledge, understanding and wisdom.
He will not disappoint you.

Collect good rules and put them into practice.

• Proverbs 14:24 The wise accumulate wisdom; fools get stupider
by the day. (The Message)

• Proverbs 2:7 He layeth up sound wisdom for the righteous:
he is a buckler to them that walk uprightly.

**Look for our book Poverty vs Wealth on Amazon
and visit our website:**

RogerBraker.com   ---   The Prosperous Life

List of Rules

Rule #1 – We Charge to "Look."
Rule #2 – We Charge for Every Trip. (As much as possible)
Rule #3 – Expect God to Give You the Right Words!
Rule #4 – Never Back Up On a Bid!
Rule #5 – Never Do Time and Materials.
Rule #6 – Avoid an Expanding Scope of Work.
Rule #7 – Don't Divide out a Bid.
Rule #8 – Never Downgrade Your Competition.
Rule #9 – Don't Work for Friends.
Rule #10 – Verify.
Rule #11 – Don't Tell People about Your Problems!
Rule #12 – Never Work for Just One Company or Client.
Rule #13 – Don't Stir the Pot.
Rule #14 – Keep How Much You Make to Yourself.
Rule #15 – Keep Your Integrity.

Rule #16 – Have Some Respect for Yourself.

Rule #17 – Don't Become Comfortable and Complacent!

Rule #18 – Practice Rephrasing Anything Questionable or Unclear.

Rule #19 – Never Look in the Windows.

Rule #20 – Be Bold When It Comes to Money.

Rule #21 – Learn Good Marketing Skills.

Rule #22 – Charge Like a Business.

Rule #23 – We Never Do A Job Hoping To Get Paid.

Rule #24 – Answer a Question with a Question.

Rule #25 – Stand up for Yourself.

Rule #26 – Never Sit in the Driveway.

Rule #27 – Leave the Key in the Lock.

Rule #28 – Establish Trust.

Rule #29 – Never Take Instructions from Anyone Other Than Who is Paying.

Rule #30 – Ask Who Is Paying for the Job, Part 1.

Rule #31 – Always Return Your Phone Calls or Reply to Text Messages Promptly.

Rule #32 – We Don't Pick up Checks!

Rule #33 – Take Care of Call Backs Immediately.

Rule #34 – Eat That Frog.

Rule #35 – Don't Stay on Hold for Too Long.

Rule #36 – Do an Extra Job Each Day.

Rule #37 – Use the 80/20 Rule.

Rule #38 – Go Get the Money!

Rule #39 – No Waiting on Third Parties to Pay Your Customer.

Rule #40 – Collect Money up Front for Parts.

Rule #41 – Call about the Bill the Next Day.

Rule #42 – Don't Work for Lawyers.

Rule #43 – Ask Who is Paying for the Job, Part 2.

Rule #44 – Tell People Up Front What the Cost is Going to Be.

Rule #45 – We Get Paid on Completion of a Commercial Job.

Rule #46 – Keep Calling!

Rule #47 – Don't Allow People to Make You Feel Guilty for Collecting.

Rule #48 – Never Accept a Beer from a Client.

Rule #49 – We Only Will Wait 10 to 15 Minutes.

Rule #50 – Only Reschedule Once.

Rule #51 – Be on Time.

Rule #52 – Never Go into Homes with Only Young Children, Especially Girls.

Rule #53 – Go Get the Work.

Rule #54 – Keep Your Foot in Both Sides of the Market.

Rule #55 – Practice Self-Development.

Rule #56 – Tell Them What to Expect.

Rule #57 – We Don't Give Discounts.

Rule #58 – Pray.

Made in the USA
Columbia, SC
30 December 2017